scene NOTES

IMAGINE & REFLECT ON YOUR KINK ADVENTURES

Copyright © 2021 by Princess Kali

All rights reserved.
Published by Erotication Publications
EroticationPublications.com

No part of this book may be reproduced, scanned, or distributed in any printed or electronic form without written permission from the copyright holder or a stated representative. To request permission or for information about bulk purchases, please email: Kali@Erotication.com

Cover design and book design by Hannah Portello-Swagel

ISBN: 978-1-7340461-7-5

CONTENTS

Welcome 1

How to Use This Workbook 2

Tips for Pacing a Scene 5

Consent 21

Imagine + Reflect 33

WELCOME

Anticipation can be the most exquisite part of any experience, and there are many benefits to thinking back on an erotic encounter, as well. Many sexual adventurers find an extra layer of enjoyment in thinking about how future kink scenes will play out and how past scenes have gone.

In many interactions, the top or dominant is the one planning the scene, but that's not the only way to approach it! As I always say, "Kink is a team sport," which is a good reminder that every player can contribute to brainstorming, planning, and considering ways to improve sexy experiences.

You don't need to use this journal for every scene (unless you want to), as both planned and spontaneous play are enjoyable for different reasons. You can use this journal casually like a diary, or with more intention as a tool for growth and connection.

Feel free to get creative! Use different color pens, highlighters, or anything else that will make this book as personal as your desires are. If you're a switch, you can color code your writing or use different colors for different partners.

The most important thing is that you have a fun and satisfying sex life that fits you, and I hope this journal helps you create exactly that!

Princess Kali
Author
Founder of KinkAcademy.com

HOW TO USE THIS WORKBOOK

The page layouts in this journal are designed to give you a framework for your writing (so you don't have to face a blank page) while also providing a lot of freedom to shape your own reflections. Use as much or as little of each page as you like.

IMAGINE

Players: Who will be part of this scene?

Roles: Are you in a power dynamic? Are you exploring roleplay?

Duration: How long is this scene going to last? Do you have any time constraints?

Environment: Where will this scene take place? Are there any special needs you have for your surroundings?

Clothing/Nudity: Is there something specific that one or more of the players should (or should not) wear?

Goal Feelings: How does each player want to feel during and after the scene?

Activities: Are there specific activities that any of the players desire?

Limits: What are each player's soft and hard limits?

Toys/Accessories: Do you need any specific toys or sexual accessories?

Storyline: Are you incorporating a roleplay scenario?

Aftercare: What are each player's needs after the scene is over? Consider what each might need immediately after as well as at a later date.

HOW TO USE THIS WORKBOOK

I recommend doing the reflection writing within three days of your scene to make sure that your memory is fresh.

REFLECT

What worked? What did you enjoy about the scene? Why was it enjoyable?

What didn't work? Did you try something new that wasn't enjoyable? Did you reach any unexpected limits, or did anything go wrong?

What do we want to do again? Is there anything from the scene that you would like to repeat in the future?

What do we want to change next time? Would an adjustment improve the experience for the future?

Additional thoughts: Are there any additional comments or insights you have about the experience?

GUIDE TO PLANNING A SCENE

What do you need to think about when planning a scene?

How long do you have to play?

What are **your goals** for the session?

How do each of you **want to feel** during/after?

How can you create **ambiance** (light, music, cleaning up)?

Will **clothing** be a factor?

Are there any **activities or toys** that *must* be included?

How much time do you need for **preparation or aftercare**?

Kinky playtime can be long and luxurious, or it can come in quick, spontaneous bursts (aka Kinky Quickies) throughout your day.

REMEMBER!
If you tend to rush, start slowly and take your time.
You don't need to speed through the experience.
When you think you've been doing something for ages, keep going for another few minutes.

GUIDE TO PLANNING A SCENE

GENERAL TIPS

- Don't try to "accomplish" too much, because pleasure is the ultimate goal, not stress.
- Choose activities that are suited to the realistic amounts of time and energy you have for a scene.
- Go at your natural pace. If you have time "left over," use it to connect in other ways.
- Remember that this is supposed to be fun, not work, so keep your spirits light and playful! If something goes "wrong," just go with the flow and see how you can adapt.

BUILD THE TIMING INTO THE SCENE

- Put an hourglass or kitchen timer in front of the bottom during impact play.
- Create a musical playlist with songs that last five minutes each.
- Have the bottom/submissive count strokes or repeat a chant.

TRANSITIONING FROM ONE ACTIVITY TO ANOTHER

- Take a break between activities. It can be good to have a little breather.
- If you're the top, use chants, mantras, and self-focused activities to keep the bottom busy while you're preparing the next activity.
- A break is still "in scene" if the bottom is given specific directions (e.g., "Take three deep breaths and drink water from my lips...").
- Repetition (doing one thing over and over again) or a Mixed Bag (going back and forth among three activities during the session) can vary the way the session "paces."

GUIDE TO PLANNING A SCENE

SIMPLE CAN BE SEXY!

- Pick no more than three activities to focus on. Less is usually better than more.
- You don't have to expend a lot of physical effort or use a bag full of toys to have a powerful scene. Focus on how you each want to feel and then explore activities that create those feelings.
- Advanced or high-intensity activities aren't necessarily better! There's pleasure to be enjoyed at every level of play, so embrace what works for you.

GET CREATIVE

- You don't need any special or expensive toys; do-it-yourself pervertables can be just as fun!
- Seek out inspiration on trusted websites or in new erotica stories. Check out the videos on KinkAcademy.com to learn a new skill or grow your perspective on a favorite way to play.
- Roleplay can be silly or serious and as intricate or basic as you want. You can use elaborate props and storylines or simply shift your energy to bring a character to life.

CONTROL THE PACING

- It's very easy to "pop" early in the session, so be sure to take your time and make every act intentional and focused so you aren't hurrying through.
- Pausing to concentrate on verbal play is a great way to both heighten and extend the scene. Usually, this enables you to continue doing something physical for a bit longer. Silence often either makes it feel like time is passing slowly or pushes us to get through our actions quickly. So, use silence for effect, but if you want to draw things out, try talking a bit more.

CONSENT

Q: What is consent?
A: Permission for something to happen.

Q: Whose responsibility is it to gain consent?
A: Everyone's!

Q: Why is consent critical?
A: It's required as part of a healthy, happy experience. It's also the law!

Q: What can affect someone's ability to consent?
A:
1) "Newthusiasm" or overconfidence
2) Low experience, understanding, or skill level
3) Drugs, alcohol, medication, or exhaustion
4) Being in "top space" or "sub space"
5) Feeling competitive with yourself or others
6) Relationship status or community standing

REMEMBER!

- Consent issues are applicable for all genders and orientations, tops and bottoms.
- Informed consent is the most critical kind of consent. Everyone must know and understand what they're agreeing to.
- Consent is the responsibility of all parties. Give/remove your consent clearly, and always ensure the consent of your partner.
- Consent doesn't have to be sexy to be important.
- Any player can withdraw consent at any time for any reason. Everyone should have a safeword and a safe gesture.
- Identify and communicate your wants, needs, and limits.
- "Forced" refers to consensual non-consent. While the energy of the scene is that the person is being "forced" so they can experience giving up responsibility for what is happening to them, they must give consent before the scene begins.

Kinksters have different ways of talking about consent and kink, using these acronyms:

SSC: Safe, Sane, and Consensual. The activities are inherently "safe" (i.e., there is no risk of significant harm).

RACK: Risk Aware Consensual Kink. The activities are not necessarily safe (i.e., there is a risk of significant harm); however, all players involved are aware of the risk.

PRICK: Personal Responsibility in Consensual Kink. Kink is certainly a team sport, but each person has a responsibility to themselves and anyone else to bring their best game, which includes communicating desires, needs, and limits.

KEY CONCEPT
The one common thread that runs through each of these risk profiles: CONSENT.

How to Withdraw Consent

The classic in the BDSM world is, of course, the use of safewords. "No" is not a safeword. **Pick something that you can remember** and say in alternate headspaces.

Be very clear. Do not just say, "No." Say, "I do not consent to this," or "I don't want this; you don't have my consent."

For tops/dominants, a good guideline is, "**If it's a maybe, it's a no.**"

If speech is restricted, **use a safe gesture**.

May your kink adventures be satisfying!

📅 DATE:

👥 PLAYERS:

📋 ROLES:

🕐 DURATION:

🛏 ENVIRONMENT:

🎭 CLOTHING / NUDITY:

🎯 GOAL FEELINGS:

🛠 ACTIVITIES:

🔗 TOYS / ACCESSORIES:

🚫 LIMITS:

SCENARIO / STORYLINE:

AFTERCARE:

NOTES:

IMAGINE

DATE:

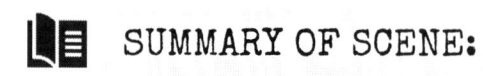

SUMMARY OF SCENE:

RATING (CIRCLE ONE):

1 2 3 4 5 6 7 8 9 10

REFLECT

👍 **WHAT WORKED?**

👎 **WHAT DIDN'T WORK?**

🔄 **WHAT DO WE WANT TO DO AGAIN?**

🔀 **WHAT DO WE WANT TO CHANGE NEXT TIME?**

💭 **ADDITIONAL THOUGHTS:**

- 📅 DATE:
- 👥 PLAYERS:
- 🪪 ROLES:
- 🕐 DURATION:
- 🛏 ENVIRONMENT:

- 🎭 CLOTHING / NUDITY:

- 🎯 GOAL FEELINGS:

- 🛏️ ACTIVITIES:

- 🔗 TOYS / ACCESSORIES:

- 🚫 LIMITS:

SCENARIO / STORYLINE:

AFTERCARE:

NOTES:

IMAGINE

DATE:

SUMMARY OF SCENE:

RATING (CIRCLE ONE):

1   2   3   4   5   6   7   8   9   10

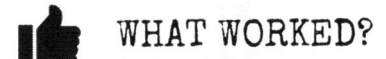

REFLECT

👍 **WHAT WORKED?**

👎 **WHAT DIDN'T WORK?**

🔄 **WHAT DO WE WANT TO DO AGAIN?**

🔀 **WHAT DO WE WANT TO CHANGE NEXT TIME?**

💭 **ADDITIONAL THOUGHTS:**

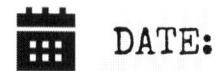

📅 DATE:

👥 PLAYERS:

📋 ROLES:

🕐 DURATION:

🛏 ENVIRONMENT:

🎭 CLOTHING / NUDITY:

🎯 GOAL FEELINGS:

💆 ACTIVITIES:

🔗 TOYS / ACCESSORIES:

🚫 LIMITS:

SCENARIO / STORYLINE:

AFTERCARE:

NOTES:

IMAGINE

DATE:

SUMMARY OF SCENE:

RATING (CIRCLE ONE):

1 2 3 4 5 6 7 8 9 10

REFLECT

👍 **WHAT WORKED?**

👎 **WHAT DIDN'T WORK?**

🔄 **WHAT DO WE WANT TO DO AGAIN?**

🔀 **WHAT DO WE WANT TO CHANGE NEXT TIME?**

💭 **ADDITIONAL THOUGHTS:**

DATE:

PLAYERS:

ROLES:

DURATION:

ENVIRONMENT:

CLOTHING / NUDITY:

GOAL FEELINGS:

ACTIVITIES:

TOYS / ACCESSORIES:

LIMITS:

SCENARIO / STORYLINE:

AFTERCARE:

NOTES:

IMAGINE

📅 DATE:

📖 SUMMARY OF SCENE:

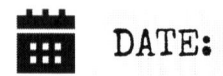

⭐ RATING (CIRCLE ONE):

    1 2 3 4 5 6 7 8 9 10

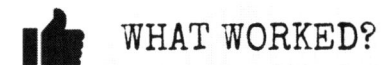

REFLECT

👍 **WHAT WORKED?**

👎 **WHAT DIDN'T WORK?**

🔄 **WHAT DO WE WANT TO DO AGAIN?**

🔀 **WHAT DO WE WANT TO CHANGE NEXT TIME?**

💭 **ADDITIONAL THOUGHTS:**

- DATE:
- PLAYERS:
- ROLES:
- DURATION:
- ENVIRONMENT:

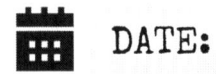

- CLOTHING / NUDITY:

- GOAL FEELINGS:

- ACTIVITIES:

- TOYS / ACCESSORIES:

- LIMITS:

IMAGINE

SCENARIO / STORYLINE:

AFTERCARE:

NOTES:

DATE:

SUMMARY OF SCENE:

RATING (CIRCLE ONE):
1 2 3 4 5 6 7 8 9 10

REFLECT

👍 **WHAT WORKED?**

👎 **WHAT DIDN'T WORK?**

🔄 **WHAT DO WE WANT TO DO AGAIN?**

🔀 **WHAT DO WE WANT TO CHANGE NEXT TIME?**

💭 **ADDITIONAL THOUGHTS:**

📅 DATE:

👥 PLAYERS:

📋 ROLES:

🕐 DURATION:

🛏 ENVIRONMENT:

🎭 CLOTHING / NUDITY:

🎯 GOAL FEELINGS:

🧗 ACTIVITIES:

🔗 TOYS / ACCESSORIES:

🚫 LIMITS:

SCENARIO / STORYLINE:

AFTERCARE:

NOTES:

IMAGINE

📅 DATE:

📖 SUMMARY OF SCENE:

⭐ RATING (CIRCLE ONE):

1   2   3   4   5   6   7   8   9   10

REFLECT

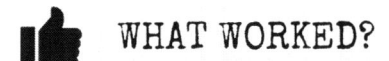

👍 **WHAT WORKED?**

👎 **WHAT DIDN'T WORK?**

🔄 **WHAT DO WE WANT TO DO AGAIN?**

🔀 **WHAT DO WE WANT TO CHANGE NEXT TIME?**

💭 **ADDITIONAL THOUGHTS:**

📅 DATE:

👥 PLAYERS:

📋 ROLES:

🕓 DURATION:

🛏 ENVIRONMENT:

🎭 CLOTHING / NUDITY:

🎯 GOAL FEELINGS:

🛠 ACTIVITIES:

🔗 TOYS / ACCESSORIES:

🚫 LIMITS:

SCENARIO / STORYLINE:

AFTERCARE:

NOTES:

IMAGINE

📅 DATE:

📖 SUMMARY OF SCENE:

⭐ RATING (CIRCLE ONE):

1 2 3 4 5 6 7 8 9 10

REFLECT

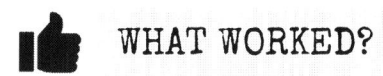

👍 **WHAT WORKED?**

👎 **WHAT DIDN'T WORK?**

🔄 **WHAT DO WE WANT TO DO AGAIN?**

🔀 **WHAT DO WE WANT TO CHANGE NEXT TIME?**

💭 **ADDITIONAL THOUGHTS:**

- DATE:
- PLAYERS:
- ROLES:
- DURATION:
- ENVIRONMENT:

- CLOTHING / NUDITY:

- GOAL FEELINGS:

- ACTIVITIES:

- TOYS / ACCESSORIES:

- LIMITS:

SCENARIO / STORYLINE:

AFTERCARE:

NOTES:

IMAGINE

📅 DATE:

📖 SUMMARY OF SCENE:

⭐ RATING (CIRCLE ONE):

1 2 3 4 5 6 7 8 9 10

REFLECT

👍 **WHAT WORKED?**

👎 **WHAT DIDN'T WORK?**

🔄 **WHAT DO WE WANT TO DO AGAIN?**

🔀 **WHAT DO WE WANT TO CHANGE NEXT TIME?**

💭 **ADDITIONAL THOUGHTS:**

- DATE:
- PLAYERS:
- ROLES:
- DURATION:
- ENVIRONMENT:

- CLOTHING / NUDITY:

- GOAL FEELINGS:

- ACTIVITIES:

- TOYS / ACCESSORIES:

- LIMITS:

SCENARIO / STORYLINE:

AFTERCARE:

NOTES:

IMAGINE

📅 DATE:

📖 SUMMARY OF SCENE:

⭐ RATING (CIRCLE ONE):

1   2   3   4   5   6   7   8   9   10

REFLECT

👍 **WHAT WORKED?**

👎 **WHAT DIDN'T WORK?**

🔄 **WHAT DO WE WANT TO DO AGAIN?**

🔀 **WHAT DO WE WANT TO CHANGE NEXT TIME?**

💬 **ADDITIONAL THOUGHTS:**

- **DATE:**
- **PLAYERS:**
- **ROLES:**
- **DURATION:**
- **ENVIRONMENT:**
- **CLOTHING / NUDITY:**
- **GOAL FEELINGS:**
- **ACTIVITIES:**
- **TOYS / ACCESSORIES:**
- **LIMITS:**

SCENARIO / STORYLINE:

AFTERCARE:

NOTES:

IMAGINE

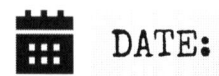

DATE:

SUMMARY OF SCENE:

RATING (CIRCLE ONE):

1   2   3   4   5   6   7   8   9   10

REFLECT

👍 **WHAT WORKED?**

👎 **WHAT DIDN'T WORK?**

🔄 **WHAT DO WE WANT TO DO AGAIN?**

🔀 **WHAT DO WE WANT TO CHANGE NEXT TIME?**

💭 **ADDITIONAL THOUGHTS:**

- DATE:
- PLAYERS:
- ROLES:
- DURATION:
- ENVIRONMENT:

- CLOTHING / NUDITY:

- GOAL FEELINGS:

- ACTIVITIES:

- TOYS / ACCESSORIES:

- LIMITS:

SCENARIO / STORYLINE:

AFTERCARE:

NOTES:

IMAGINE

DATE:

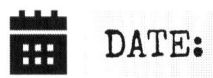

SUMMARY OF SCENE:

RATING (CIRCLE ONE):

1　2　3　4　5　6　7　8　9　10

REFLECT

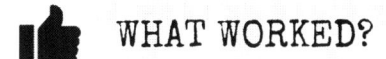

👍 **WHAT WORKED?**

👎 **WHAT DIDN'T WORK?**

🔄 **WHAT DO WE WANT TO DO AGAIN?**

🔀 **WHAT DO WE WANT TO CHANGE NEXT TIME?**

💭 **ADDITIONAL THOUGHTS:**

- 📅 **DATE:**
- 👥 **PLAYERS:**
- 📋 **ROLES:**
- 🕐 **DURATION:**
- 🛏 **ENVIRONMENT:**

- 🎭 **CLOTHING / NUDITY:**

- 🎯 **GOAL FEELINGS:**

- **ACTIVITIES:**

- 🔗 **TOYS / ACCESSORIES:**

- 🚫 **LIMITS:**

SCENARIO / STORYLINE:

AFTERCARE:

NOTES:

IMAGINE

📅 DATE:

📖 SUMMARY OF SCENE:

⭐ RATING (CIRCLE ONE):

1 2 3 4 5 6 7 8 9 10

REFLECT

👍 **WHAT WORKED?**

👎 **WHAT DIDN'T WORK?**

🔄 **WHAT DO WE WANT TO DO AGAIN?**

🔀 **WHAT DO WE WANT TO CHANGE NEXT TIME?**

💭 **ADDITIONAL THOUGHTS:**

DATE:

PLAYERS:

ROLES:

DURATION:

ENVIRONMENT:

CLOTHING / NUDITY:

GOAL FEELINGS:

ACTIVITIES:

TOYS / ACCESSORIES:

LIMITS:

SCENARIO / STORYLINE:

AFTERCARE:

NOTES:

IMAGINE

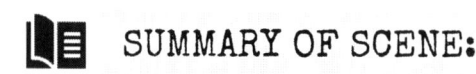

📅 DATE:

📖 SUMMARY OF SCENE:

⭐ RATING (CIRCLE ONE):

1   2   3   4   5   6   7   8   9   10

REFLECT

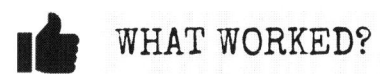

👍 **WHAT WORKED?**

👎 **WHAT DIDN'T WORK?**

🔄 **WHAT DO WE WANT TO DO AGAIN?**

🔀 **WHAT DO WE WANT TO CHANGE NEXT TIME?**

💭 **ADDITIONAL THOUGHTS:**

- **DATE:**
- **PLAYERS:**
- **ROLES:**
- **DURATION:**
- **ENVIRONMENT:**

- **CLOTHING / NUDITY:**

- **GOAL FEELINGS:**

- **ACTIVITIES:**

- **TOYS / ACCESSORIES:**

- **LIMITS:**

SCENARIO / STORYLINE:

AFTERCARE:

NOTES:

IMAGINE

📅 DATE:

📖 SUMMARY OF SCENE:

⭐ RATING (CIRCLE ONE):

1   2   3   4   5   6   7   8   9   10

REFLECT

👍 **WHAT WORKED?**

👎 **WHAT DIDN'T WORK?**

🔄 **WHAT DO WE WANT TO DO AGAIN?**

🔀 **WHAT DO WE WANT TO CHANGE NEXT TIME?**

💭 **ADDITIONAL THOUGHTS:**

📅 DATE:

👥 PLAYERS:

🪪 ROLES:

🕐 DURATION:

🛏 ENVIRONMENT:

🎭 CLOTHING / NUDITY:

🎯 GOAL FEELINGS:

🤸 ACTIVITIES:

🧸 TOYS / ACCESSORIES:

🚫 LIMITS:

SCENARIO / STORYLINE:

AFTERCARE:

NOTES:

IMAGINE

DATE:

SUMMARY OF SCENE:

RATING (CIRCLE ONE):

1   2   3   4   5   6   7   8   9   10

REFLECT

👍 **WHAT WORKED?**

👎 **WHAT DIDN'T WORK?**

🔄 **WHAT DO WE WANT TO DO AGAIN?**

🔀 **WHAT DO WE WANT TO CHANGE NEXT TIME?**

💭 **ADDITIONAL THOUGHTS:**

DATE:

PLAYERS:

ROLES:

DURATION:

ENVIRONMENT:

CLOTHING / NUDITY:

GOAL FEELINGS:

ACTIVITIES:

TOYS / ACCESSORIES:

LIMITS:

SCENARIO / STORYLINE:

AFTERCARE:

NOTES:

IMAGINE

DATE:

SUMMARY OF SCENE:

RATING (CIRCLE ONE):

1   2   3   4   5   6   7   8   9   10

👍 WHAT WORKED?

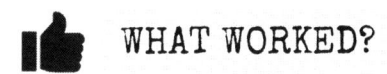

👎 WHAT DIDN'T WORK?

🔄 WHAT DO WE WANT TO DO AGAIN?

🔀 WHAT DO WE WANT TO CHANGE NEXT TIME?

💭 ADDITIONAL THOUGHTS:

REFLECT

📅 DATE:

👥 PLAYERS:

🪪 ROLES:

🕐 DURATION:

🛏 ENVIRONMENT:

🎭 CLOTHING / NUDITY:

🎯 GOAL FEELINGS:

💆 ACTIVITIES:

🔗 TOYS / ACCESSORIES:

🚫 LIMITS:

SCENARIO / STORYLINE:

AFTERCARE:

NOTES:

IMAGINE

DATE:

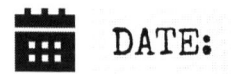

SUMMARY OF SCENE:

RATING (CIRCLE ONE):

1 2 3 4 5 6 7 8 9 10

REFLECT

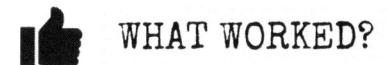

👍 **WHAT WORKED?**

👎 **WHAT DIDN'T WORK?**

🔄 **WHAT DO WE WANT TO DO AGAIN?**

🔀 **WHAT DO WE WANT TO CHANGE NEXT TIME?**

💭 **ADDITIONAL THOUGHTS:**

- DATE:
- PLAYERS:
- ROLES:
- DURATION:
- ENVIRONMENT:

- CLOTHING / NUDITY:

- GOAL FEELINGS:

- ACTIVITIES:

- TOYS / ACCESSORIES:

- LIMITS:

SCENARIO / STORYLINE:

AFTERCARE:

NOTES:

IMAGINE

DATE:

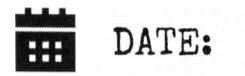

SUMMARY OF SCENE:

RATING (CIRCLE ONE):

   1   2   3   4   5   6   7   8   9   10

REFLECT

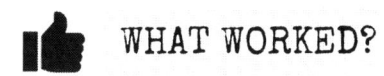

👍 **WHAT WORKED?**

👎 **WHAT DIDN'T WORK?**

🔄 **WHAT DO WE WANT TO DO AGAIN?**

🔀 **WHAT DO WE WANT TO CHANGE NEXT TIME?**

💭 **ADDITIONAL THOUGHTS:**

DATE:

PLAYERS:

ROLES:

DURATION:

ENVIRONMENT:

CLOTHING / NUDITY:

GOAL FEELINGS:

ACTIVITIES:

TOYS / ACCESSORIES:

LIMITS:

SCENARIO / STORYLINE:

AFTERCARE:

NOTES:

IMAGINE

DATE:

SUMMARY OF SCENE:

RATING (CIRCLE ONE):

1   2   3   4   5   6   7   8   9   10

REFLECT

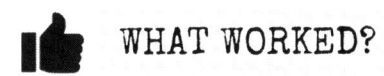

👍 **WHAT WORKED?**

👎 **WHAT DIDN'T WORK?**

🔄 **WHAT DO WE WANT TO DO AGAIN?**

🔀 **WHAT DO WE WANT TO CHANGE NEXT TIME?**

💭 **ADDITIONAL THOUGHTS:**

DATE:

PLAYERS:

ROLES:

DURATION:

ENVIRONMENT:

CLOTHING / NUDITY:

GOAL FEELINGS:

ACTIVITIES:

TOYS / ACCESSORIES:

LIMITS:

IMAGINE

SCENARIO / STORYLINE:

AFTERCARE:

NOTES:

📅 **DATE:**

📖 **SUMMARY OF SCENE:**

⭐ **RATING (CIRCLE ONE):**

1   2   3   4   5   6   7   8   9   10

REFLECT

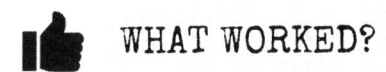

👍 **WHAT WORKED?**

👎 **WHAT DIDN'T WORK?**

🔄 **WHAT DO WE WANT TO DO AGAIN?**

🔀 **WHAT DO WE WANT TO CHANGE NEXT TIME?**

💭 **ADDITIONAL THOUGHTS:**

📅 DATE:

👥 PLAYERS:

📋 ROLES:

🕐 DURATION:

🛏️ ENVIRONMENT:

🎭 CLOTHING / NUDITY:

🎯 GOAL FEELINGS:

💆 ACTIVITIES:

🔗 TOYS / ACCESSORIES:

🚫 LIMITS:

SCENARIO / STORYLINE:

AFTERCARE:

NOTES:

IMAGINE

📅 DATE:

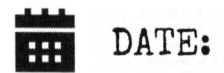

📖 SUMMARY OF SCENE:

⭐ RATING (CIRCLE ONE):

1   2   3   4   5   6   7   8   9   10

👍 WHAT WORKED?

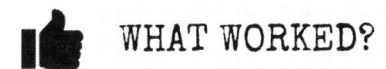

👎 WHAT DIDN'T WORK?

🔄 WHAT DO WE WANT TO DO AGAIN?

🔀 WHAT DO WE WANT TO CHANGE NEXT TIME?

💭 ADDITIONAL THOUGHTS:

REFLECT

📅 DATE:

👥 PLAYERS:

🪪 ROLES:

🕐 DURATION:

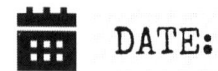

🛏️ ENVIRONMENT:

🎭 CLOTHING / NUDITY:

🎯 GOAL FEELINGS:

ACTIVITIES:

🔗 TOYS / ACCESSORIES:

🚫 LIMITS:

SCENARIO / STORYLINE:

AFTERCARE:

NOTES:

IMAGINE

📅 DATE:

📖 SUMMARY OF SCENE:

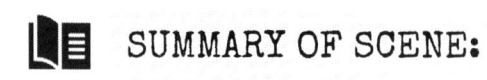

⭐ RATING (CIRCLE ONE):

    1 2 3 4 5 6 7 8 9 10

REFLECT

👍 **WHAT WORKED?**

👎 **WHAT DIDN'T WORK?**

🔄 **WHAT DO WE WANT TO DO AGAIN?**

🔀 **WHAT DO WE WANT TO CHANGE NEXT TIME?**

💭 **ADDITIONAL THOUGHTS:**

📅 DATE:

👥 PLAYERS:

📋 ROLES:

🕐 DURATION:

🛏 ENVIRONMENT:

🎭 CLOTHING / NUDITY:

🎯 GOAL FEELINGS:

ACTIVITIES:

🔗 TOYS / ACCESSORIES:

🚫 LIMITS:

SCENARIO / STORYLINE:

AFTERCARE:

NOTES:

IMAGINE

📅 DATE:

📖 SUMMARY OF SCENE:

⭐ RATING (CIRCLE ONE):

1   2   3   4   5   6   7   8   9   10

REFLECT

👍 **WHAT WORKED?**

👎 **WHAT DIDN'T WORK?**

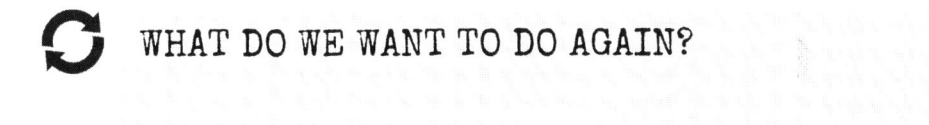

🔄 **WHAT DO WE WANT TO DO AGAIN?**

🔀 **WHAT DO WE WANT TO CHANGE NEXT TIME?**

💭 **ADDITIONAL THOUGHTS:**

📅 DATE:

👥 PLAYERS:

📋 ROLES:

🕐 DURATION:

🛏 ENVIRONMENT:

🎭 CLOTHING / NUDITY:

🎯 GOAL FEELINGS:

🛠 ACTIVITIES:

⏱ TOYS / ACCESSORIES:

🚫 LIMITS:

SCENARIO / STORYLINE:

AFTERCARE:

NOTES:

IMAGINE

📅 DATE:

📖 SUMMARY OF SCENE:

⭐ RATING (CIRCLE ONE):

1   2   3   4   5   6   7   8   9   10

REFLECT

👍 **WHAT WORKED?**

👎 **WHAT DIDN'T WORK?**

🔄 **WHAT DO WE WANT TO DO AGAIN?**

🔀 **WHAT DO WE WANT TO CHANGE NEXT TIME?**

💬 **ADDITIONAL THOUGHTS:**

📅 DATE:

👥 PLAYERS:

📇 ROLES:

🕐 DURATION:

🛏 ENVIRONMENT:

🎭 CLOTHING / NUDITY:

🎯 GOAL FEELINGS:

🛐 ACTIVITIES:

🔗 TOYS / ACCESSORIES:

🚫 LIMITS:

SCENARIO / STORYLINE:

AFTERCARE:

NOTES:

IMAGINE

📅 DATE:

📖 SUMMARY OF SCENE:

⭐ RATING (CIRCLE ONE):

1   2   3   4   5   6   7   8   9   10

REFLECT

👍 **WHAT WORKED?**

👎 **WHAT DIDN'T WORK?**

🔄 **WHAT DO WE WANT TO DO AGAIN?**

🔀 **WHAT DO WE WANT TO CHANGE NEXT TIME?**

💭 **ADDITIONAL THOUGHTS:**

📅 DATE:

👥 PLAYERS:

📋 ROLES:

🕒 DURATION:

🛏 ENVIRONMENT:

🎭 CLOTHING / NUDITY:

🎯 GOAL FEELINGS:

💆 ACTIVITIES:

🔗 TOYS / ACCESSORIES:

🚫 LIMITS:

SCENARIO / STORYLINE:

AFTERCARE:

NOTES:

IMAGINE

📅 DATE:

📖 SUMMARY OF SCENE:

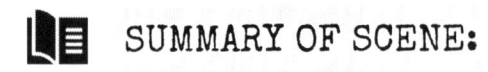

⭐ RATING (CIRCLE ONE):

1   2   3   4   5   6   7   8   9   10

REFLECT

👍 **WHAT WORKED?**

👎 **WHAT DIDN'T WORK?**

🔄 **WHAT DO WE WANT TO DO AGAIN?**

🔀 **WHAT DO WE WANT TO CHANGE NEXT TIME?**

💭 **ADDITIONAL THOUGHTS:**

📅 DATE:

👥 PLAYERS:

📇 ROLES:

🕐 DURATION:

🛏 ENVIRONMENT:

🎭 CLOTHING / NUDITY:

🎯 GOAL FEELINGS:

💆 ACTIVITIES:

🔗 TOYS / ACCESSORIES:

🚫 LIMITS:

IMAGINE

SCENARIO / STORYLINE:

AFTERCARE:

NOTES:

DATE:

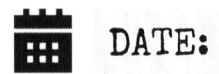

SUMMARY OF SCENE:

RATING (CIRCLE ONE):

1 2 3 4 5 6 7 8 9 10

REFLECT

👍 **WHAT WORKED?**

👎 **WHAT DIDN'T WORK?**

🔄 **WHAT DO WE WANT TO DO AGAIN?**

🔀 **WHAT DO WE WANT TO CHANGE NEXT TIME?**

💭 **ADDITIONAL THOUGHTS:**

📅 DATE:

👥 PLAYERS:

🪪 ROLES:

🕒 DURATION:

🛏️ ENVIRONMENT:

🎭 CLOTHING / NUDITY:

🎯 GOAL FEELINGS:

💆 ACTIVITIES:

🔗 TOYS / ACCESSORIES:

🚫 LIMITS:

SCENARIO / STORYLINE:

AFTERCARE:

NOTES:

IMAGINE

📅 DATE:

📖 SUMMARY OF SCENE:

⭐ RATING (CIRCLE ONE):

    1 2 3 4 5 6 7 8 9 10

REFLECT

👍 **WHAT WORKED?**

👎 **WHAT DIDN'T WORK?**

🔄 **WHAT DO WE WANT TO DO AGAIN?**

🔀 **WHAT DO WE WANT TO CHANGE NEXT TIME?**

💭 **ADDITIONAL THOUGHTS:**

- **DATE:**
- **PLAYERS:**
- **ROLES:**
- **DURATION:**
- **ENVIRONMENT:**
- **CLOTHING / NUDITY:**
- **GOAL FEELINGS:**
- **ACTIVITIES:**
- **TOYS / ACCESSORIES:**
- **LIMITS:**

SCENARIO / STORYLINE:

AFTERCARE:

NOTES:

IMAGINE

📅 DATE:

📖 SUMMARY OF SCENE:

⭐ RATING (CIRCLE ONE):

1　2　3　4　5　6　7　8　9　10

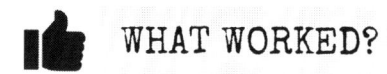

REFLECT

👍 **WHAT WORKED?**

👎 **WHAT DIDN'T WORK?**

🔄 **WHAT DO WE WANT TO DO AGAIN?**

🔀 **WHAT DO WE WANT TO CHANGE NEXT TIME?**

💭 **ADDITIONAL THOUGHTS:**

DATE:

PLAYERS:

ROLES:

DURATION:

ENVIRONMENT:

CLOTHING / NUDITY:

GOAL FEELINGS:

ACTIVITIES:

TOYS / ACCESSORIES:

LIMITS:

SCENARIO / STORYLINE:

AFTERCARE:

NOTES:

IMAGINE

📅 DATE:

📖 SUMMARY OF SCENE:

⭐ RATING (CIRCLE ONE):

    1 2 3 4 5 6 7 8 9 10

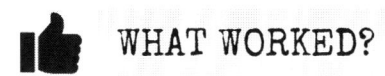

REFLECT

👍 **WHAT WORKED?**

👎 **WHAT DIDN'T WORK?**

🔄 **WHAT DO WE WANT TO DO AGAIN?**

🔀 **WHAT DO WE WANT TO CHANGE NEXT TIME?**

💭 **ADDITIONAL THOUGHTS:**

- 📅 DATE:
- 👥 PLAYERS:
- 📇 ROLES:
- 🕐 DURATION:
- 🛏 ENVIRONMENT:

- 🎭 CLOTHING / NUDITY:

- 🎯 GOAL FEELINGS:

- 🛋 ACTIVITIES:

- 🔗 TOYS / ACCESSORIES:

- 🚫 LIMITS:

SCENARIO / STORYLINE:

AFTERCARE:

NOTES:

IMAGINE

📅 DATE:

📖 SUMMARY OF SCENE:

⭐ RATING (CIRCLE ONE):

1   2   3   4   5   6   7   8   9   10

REFLECT

👍 **WHAT WORKED?**

👎 **WHAT DIDN'T WORK?**

🔄 **WHAT DO WE WANT TO DO AGAIN?**

🔀 **WHAT DO WE WANT TO CHANGE NEXT TIME?**

💭 **ADDITIONAL THOUGHTS:**

📅 DATE:

👥 PLAYERS:

📋 ROLES:

🕐 DURATION:

🛏 ENVIRONMENT:

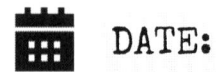

🎭 CLOTHING / NUDITY:

🎯 GOAL FEELINGS:

🤸 ACTIVITIES:

🔗 TOYS / ACCESSORIES:

🚫 LIMITS:

SCENARIO / STORYLINE:

AFTERCARE:

NOTES:

IMAGINE

DATE:

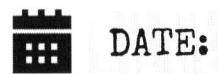

SUMMARY OF SCENE:

RATING (CIRCLE ONE):

1 2 3 4 5 6 7 8 9 10

REFLECT

👍 **WHAT WORKED?**

👎 **WHAT DIDN'T WORK?**

🔄 **WHAT DO WE WANT TO DO AGAIN?**

🔀 **WHAT DO WE WANT TO CHANGE NEXT TIME?**

💭 **ADDITIONAL THOUGHTS:**

DATE:

PLAYERS:

ROLES:

DURATION:

ENVIRONMENT:

CLOTHING / NUDITY:

GOAL FEELINGS:

ACTIVITIES:

TOYS / ACCESSORIES:

LIMITS:

SCENARIO / STORYLINE:

AFTERCARE:

NOTES:

IMAGINE

📅 DATE:

📖 SUMMARY OF SCENE:

⭐ RATING (CIRCLE ONE):

     1 2 3 4 5 6 7 8 9 10

REFLECT

👍 **WHAT WORKED?**

👎 **WHAT DIDN'T WORK?**

🔄 **WHAT DO WE WANT TO DO AGAIN?**

🔀 **WHAT DO WE WANT TO CHANGE NEXT TIME?**

💭 **ADDITIONAL THOUGHTS:**

- DATE:
- PLAYERS:
- ROLES:
- DURATION:
- ENVIRONMENT:

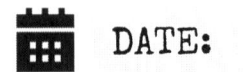

- CLOTHING / NUDITY:

- GOAL FEELINGS:

- ACTIVITIES:

- TOYS / ACCESSORIES:

- LIMITS:

SCENARIO / STORYLINE:

AFTERCARE:

NOTES:

IMAGINE

📅 DATE:

📖 SUMMARY OF SCENE:

⭐ RATING (CIRCLE ONE):

    1   2   3   4   5   6   7   8   9   10

REFLECT

👍 **WHAT WORKED?**

👎 **WHAT DIDN'T WORK?**

🔄 **WHAT DO WE WANT TO DO AGAIN?**

🔀 **WHAT DO WE WANT TO CHANGE NEXT TIME?**

💭 **ADDITIONAL THOUGHTS:**

- 📅 DATE:
- 👥 PLAYERS:
- 📋 ROLES:
- 🕐 DURATION:
- 🛏 ENVIRONMENT:

- 🎭 CLOTHING / NUDITY:

- 🎯 GOAL FEELINGS:

- 🧎 ACTIVITIES:

- 🔗 TOYS / ACCESSORIES:

- 🚫 LIMITS:

SCENARIO / STORYLINE:

AFTERCARE:

NOTES:

IMAGINE

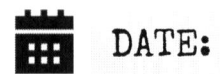

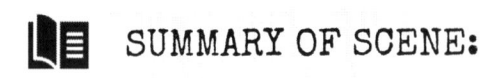

DATE:

SUMMARY OF SCENE:

RATING (CIRCLE ONE):

1   2   3   4   5   6   7   8   9   10

REFLECT

👍 **WHAT WORKED?**

👎 **WHAT DIDN'T WORK?**

🔄 **WHAT DO WE WANT TO DO AGAIN?**

🔀 **WHAT DO WE WANT TO CHANGE NEXT TIME?**

💭 **ADDITIONAL THOUGHTS:**

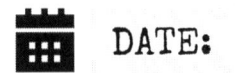

📅 DATE:

👥 PLAYERS:

📋 ROLES:

🕒 DURATION:

🛏 ENVIRONMENT:

🎭 CLOTHING / NUDITY:

🎯 GOAL FEELINGS:

💆 ACTIVITIES:

🔗 TOYS / ACCESSORIES:

🚫 LIMITS:

SCENARIO / STORYLINE:

AFTERCARE:

NOTES:

IMAGINE

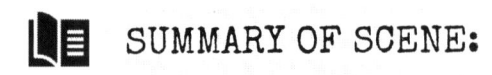

📅 DATE:

📖 SUMMARY OF SCENE:

⭐ RATING (CIRCLE ONE):

     1 2 3 4 5 6 7 8 9 10

REFLECT

👍 **WHAT WORKED?**

👎 **WHAT DIDN'T WORK?**

🔄 **WHAT DO WE WANT TO DO AGAIN?**

🔀 **WHAT DO WE WANT TO CHANGE NEXT TIME?**

💭 **ADDITIONAL THOUGHTS:**

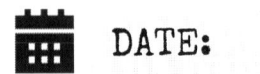

📅 DATE:

👥 PLAYERS:

📇 ROLES:

🕒 DURATION:

🛏️ ENVIRONMENT:

🎭 CLOTHING / NUDITY:

🎯 GOAL FEELINGS:

🛌 ACTIVITIES:

🔗 TOYS / ACCESSORIES:

🚫 LIMITS:

SCENARIO / STORYLINE:

AFTERCARE:

NOTES:

IMAGINE

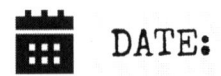

📅 DATE:

📖 SUMMARY OF SCENE:

⭐ RATING (CIRCLE ONE):

1 2 3 4 5 6 7 8 9 10

REFLECT

👍 **WHAT WORKED?**

👎 **WHAT DIDN'T WORK?**

🔄 **WHAT DO WE WANT TO DO AGAIN?**

🔀 **WHAT DO WE WANT TO CHANGE NEXT TIME?**

💭 **ADDITIONAL THOUGHTS:**

- DATE:
- PLAYERS:
- ROLES:
- DURATION:
- ENVIRONMENT:

- CLOTHING / NUDITY:

- GOAL FEELINGS:

- ACTIVITIES:

- TOYS / ACCESSORIES:

- LIMITS:

IMAGINE

SCENARIO / STORYLINE:

AFTERCARE:

NOTES:

📅 DATE:

📖 SUMMARY OF SCENE:

⭐ RATING (CIRCLE ONE):

1 2 3 4 5 6 7 8 9 10

REFLECT

👍 **WHAT WORKED?**

👎 **WHAT DIDN'T WORK?**

🔄 **WHAT DO WE WANT TO DO AGAIN?**

🔀 **WHAT DO WE WANT TO CHANGE NEXT TIME?**

💭 **ADDITIONAL THOUGHTS:**

📅 DATE:

👥 PLAYERS:

📇 ROLES:

🕐 DURATION:

🛏 ENVIRONMENT:

🎭 CLOTHING / NUDITY:

🎯 GOAL FEELINGS:

🤸 ACTIVITIES:

🔗 TOYS / ACCESSORIES:

🚫 LIMITS:

IMAGINE

SCENARIO / STORYLINE:

AFTERCARE:

NOTES:

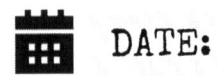

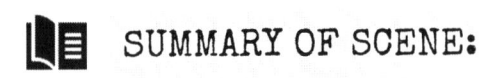

DATE:

SUMMARY OF SCENE:

RATING (CIRCLE ONE):

1   2   3   4   5   6   7   8   9   10

REFLECT

👍 **WHAT WORKED?**

👎 **WHAT DIDN'T WORK?**

🔄 **WHAT DO WE WANT TO DO AGAIN?**

🔀 **WHAT DO WE WANT TO CHANGE NEXT TIME?**

💭 **ADDITIONAL THOUGHTS:**

- DATE:
- PLAYERS:
- ROLES:
- DURATION:
- ENVIRONMENT:

- CLOTHING / NUDITY:

- GOAL FEELINGS:

- ACTIVITIES:

- TOYS / ACCESSORIES:

- LIMITS:

SCENARIO / STORYLINE:

AFTERCARE:

NOTES:

IMAGINE

📅 DATE:

📖 SUMMARY OF SCENE:

⭐ RATING (CIRCLE ONE):

    1 2 3 4 5 6 7 8 9 10

REFLECT

👍 **WHAT WORKED?**

👎 **WHAT DIDN'T WORK?**

🔄 **WHAT DO WE WANT TO DO AGAIN?**

🔀 **WHAT DO WE WANT TO CHANGE NEXT TIME?**

💭 **ADDITIONAL THOUGHTS:**

DATE:

PLAYERS:

ROLES:

DURATION:

ENVIRONMENT:

CLOTHING / NUDITY:

GOAL FEELINGS:

ACTIVITIES:

TOYS / ACCESSORIES:

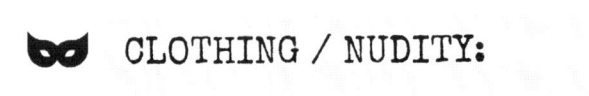

LIMITS:

SCENARIO / STORYLINE:

AFTERCARE:

NOTES:

IMAGINE

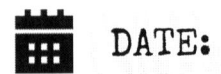

📅 DATE:

📖 SUMMARY OF SCENE:

⭐ RATING (CIRCLE ONE):

    1   2   3   4   5   6   7   8   9   10

REFLECT

👍 **WHAT WORKED?**

👎 **WHAT DIDN'T WORK?**

🔄 **WHAT DO WE WANT TO DO AGAIN?**

🔀 **WHAT DO WE WANT TO CHANGE NEXT TIME?**

💭 **ADDITIONAL THOUGHTS:**

- DATE:
- PLAYERS:
- ROLES:
- DURATION:
- ENVIRONMENT:

- CLOTHING / NUDITY:

- GOAL FEELINGS:

- ACTIVITIES:

- TOYS / ACCESSORIES:

- LIMITS:

SCENARIO / STORYLINE:

AFTERCARE:

NOTES:

IMAGINE

📅 DATE:

📖 SUMMARY OF SCENE:

⭐ RATING (CIRCLE ONE):

      1   2   3   4   5   6   7   8   9   10

REFLECT

👍 **WHAT WORKED?**

👎 **WHAT DIDN'T WORK?**

🔄 **WHAT DO WE WANT TO DO AGAIN?**

🔀 **WHAT DO WE WANT TO CHANGE NEXT TIME?**

💭 **ADDITIONAL THOUGHTS:**

📅 DATE:

👥 PLAYERS:

📇 ROLES:

🕒 DURATION:

🛏 ENVIRONMENT:

🎭 CLOTHING / NUDITY:

🎯 GOAL FEELINGS:

🧎 ACTIVITIES:

🔗 TOYS / ACCESSORIES:

🚫 LIMITS:

SCENARIO / STORYLINE:

AFTERCARE:

NOTES:

IMAGINE

DATE:

SUMMARY OF SCENE:

RATING (CIRCLE ONE):

1 2 3 4 5 6 7 8 9 10

REFLECT

👍 **WHAT WORKED?**

👎 **WHAT DIDN'T WORK?**

🔄 **WHAT DO WE WANT TO DO AGAIN?**

🔀 **WHAT DO WE WANT TO CHANGE NEXT TIME?**

💭 **ADDITIONAL THOUGHTS:**

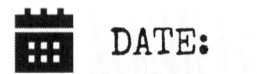

DATE:

PLAYERS:

ROLES:

DURATION:

ENVIRONMENT:

CLOTHING / NUDITY:

GOAL FEELINGS:

ACTIVITIES:

TOYS / ACCESSORIES:

LIMITS:

SCENARIO / STORYLINE:

AFTERCARE:

NOTES:

IMAGINE

📅 DATE:

📖 SUMMARY OF SCENE:

⭐ RATING (CIRCLE ONE):

    1   2   3   4   5   6   7   8   9   10

REFLECT

👍 **WHAT WORKED?**

👎 **WHAT DIDN'T WORK?**

🔄 **WHAT DO WE WANT TO DO AGAIN?**

🔀 **WHAT DO WE WANT TO CHANGE NEXT TIME?**

💭 **ADDITIONAL THOUGHTS:**

DATE:

PLAYERS:

ROLES:

DURATION:

ENVIRONMENT:

CLOTHING / NUDITY:

GOAL FEELINGS:

ACTIVITIES:

TOYS / ACCESSORIES:

LIMITS:

IMAGINE

SCENARIO / STORYLINE:

AFTERCARE:

NOTES:

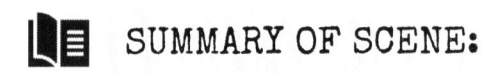

📅 DATE:

📖 SUMMARY OF SCENE:

⭐ RATING (CIRCLE ONE):

1   2   3   4   5   6   7   8   9   10

REFLECT

👍 **WHAT WORKED?**

👎 **WHAT DIDN'T WORK?**

🔄 **WHAT DO WE WANT TO DO AGAIN?**

🔀 **WHAT DO WE WANT TO CHANGE NEXT TIME?**

💭 **ADDITIONAL THOUGHTS:**

- DATE:
- PLAYERS:
- ROLES:
- DURATION:
- ENVIRONMENT:
- CLOTHING / NUDITY:
- GOAL FEELINGS:
- ACTIVITIES:
- TOYS / ACCESSORIES:
- LIMITS:

SCENARIO / STORYLINE:

AFTERCARE:

NOTES:

IMAGINE

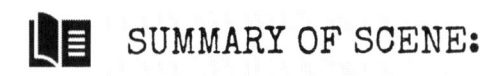

📅 DATE:

📖 SUMMARY OF SCENE:

⭐ RATING (CIRCLE ONE):

    1   2   3   4   5   6   7   8   9   10

REFLECT

👍 **WHAT WORKED?**

👎 **WHAT DIDN'T WORK?**

🔄 **WHAT DO WE WANT TO DO AGAIN?**

🔀 **WHAT DO WE WANT TO CHANGE NEXT TIME?**

💬 **ADDITIONAL THOUGHTS:**

DATE:

PLAYERS:

ROLES:

DURATION:

ENVIRONMENT:

CLOTHING / NUDITY:

GOAL FEELINGS:

ACTIVITIES:

TOYS / ACCESSORIES:

LIMITS:

SCENARIO / STORYLINE:

AFTERCARE:

NOTES:

IMAGINE

DATE:

SUMMARY OF SCENE:

RATING (CIRCLE ONE):

1   2   3   4   5   6   7   8   9   10

REFLECT

👍 **WHAT WORKED?**

👎 **WHAT DIDN'T WORK?**

🔄 **WHAT DO WE WANT TO DO AGAIN?**

🔀 **WHAT DO WE WANT TO CHANGE NEXT TIME?**

💭 **ADDITIONAL THOUGHTS:**

- DATE:
- PLAYERS:
- ROLES:
- DURATION:
- ENVIRONMENT:

- CLOTHING / NUDITY:

- GOAL FEELINGS:

- ACTIVITIES:

- TOYS / ACCESSORIES:

- LIMITS:

SCENARIO / STORYLINE:

AFTERCARE:

NOTES:

IMAGINE

📅 DATE:

📖 SUMMARY OF SCENE:

⭐ RATING (CIRCLE ONE):

1   2   3   4   5   6   7   8   9   10

REFLECT

👍 **WHAT WORKED?**

👎 **WHAT DIDN'T WORK?**

🔄 **WHAT DO WE WANT TO DO AGAIN?**

🔀 **WHAT DO WE WANT TO CHANGE NEXT TIME?**

💭 **ADDITIONAL THOUGHTS:**

📅 DATE:

👥 PLAYERS:

📇 ROLES:

🕒 DURATION:

🛏 ENVIRONMENT:

🎭 CLOTHING / NUDITY:

🎯 GOAL FEELINGS:

🤸 ACTIVITIES:

🔗 TOYS / ACCESSORIES:

🚫 LIMITS:

SCENARIO / STORYLINE:

AFTERCARE:

NOTES:

IMAGINE

DATE:

SUMMARY OF SCENE:

RATING (CIRCLE ONE):

1   2   3   4   5   6   7   8   9   10

REFLECT

👍 **WHAT WORKED?**

👎 **WHAT DIDN'T WORK?**

🔄 **WHAT DO WE WANT TO DO AGAIN?**

🔀 **WHAT DO WE WANT TO CHANGE NEXT TIME?**

💭 **ADDITIONAL THOUGHTS:**

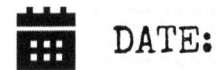

- **DATE:**
- **PLAYERS:**
- **ROLES:**
- **DURATION:**
- **ENVIRONMENT:**
- **CLOTHING / NUDITY:**
- **GOAL FEELINGS:**
- **ACTIVITIES:**
- **TOYS / ACCESSORIES:**
- **LIMITS:**

SCENARIO / STORYLINE:

AFTERCARE:

NOTES:

IMAGINE

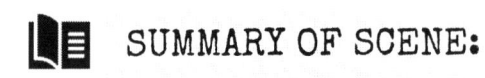

📅 DATE:

📖 SUMMARY OF SCENE:

⭐ RATING (CIRCLE ONE):

1   2   3   4   5   6   7   8   9   10

REFLECT

👍 **WHAT WORKED?**

👎 **WHAT DIDN'T WORK?**

🔄 **WHAT DO WE WANT TO DO AGAIN?**

🔀 **WHAT DO WE WANT TO CHANGE NEXT TIME?**

💭 **ADDITIONAL THOUGHTS:**

DATE:

PLAYERS:

ROLES:

DURATION:

ENVIRONMENT:

CLOTHING / NUDITY:

GOAL FEELINGS:

ACTIVITIES:

TOYS / ACCESSORIES:

LIMITS:

SCENARIO / STORYLINE:

AFTERCARE:

NOTES:

IMAGINE

📅 DATE:

📖 SUMMARY OF SCENE:

⭐ RATING (CIRCLE ONE):

1   2   3   4   5   6   7   8   9   10

REFLECT

👍 WHAT WORKED?

👎 WHAT DIDN'T WORK?

🔄 WHAT DO WE WANT TO DO AGAIN?

🔀 WHAT DO WE WANT TO CHANGE NEXT TIME?

💭 ADDITIONAL THOUGHTS:

📅 DATE:

👥 PLAYERS:

📇 ROLES:

🕐 DURATION:

🛏 ENVIRONMENT:

🎭 CLOTHING / NUDITY:

🎯 GOAL FEELINGS:

🛠 ACTIVITIES:

🔗 TOYS / ACCESSORIES:

🚫 LIMITS:

SCENARIO / STORYLINE:

AFTERCARE:

NOTES:

IMAGINE

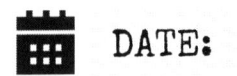

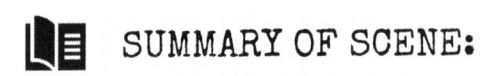

📅 DATE:

📖 SUMMARY OF SCENE:

⭐ RATING (CIRCLE ONE):

    1 2 3 4 5 6 7 8 9 10

👍 WHAT WORKED?

👎 WHAT DIDN'T WORK?

🔄 WHAT DO WE WANT TO DO AGAIN?

🔀 WHAT DO WE WANT TO CHANGE NEXT TIME?

💭 ADDITIONAL THOUGHTS:

REFLECT

Check out

SceneNotesJournal.com

for related products and additional resources.

Ready, Kink, Go! – Negotiation Deck
Kink Talk – Discussion Prompts
365 Days of Kink – Journal
The Yes, No, Maybe Workbook

MEET THE AUTHOR

Princess Kali is the founder of Kink Academy, a lifelong entrepreneur, and a relentless creator.

She's also the author of:

- Enough to Make You Blush: Exploring Erotic Humiliation
- Authentic Kink
- Making Bank

Kali's greatest joy is teaching kink classes and helping kinksters and all sexual adventurers have safer, more satisfying, creative, and joyful experiences.

KINK ACADEMY

You've grown up, and so should your sex education.

Kink Academy is a comprehensive library of sex-ed videos for adventurous, consenting adults. Whether you're new to kink or an experienced player, there's something for everyone to learn on Kink Academy.

With over 2,000 sex-ed videos and over 150 sexuality educators, the Kink Academy Team works with sex, kink, gender, and relationship experts from around the world to present the most diverse and experienced voices possible for your ongoing sexual education.

KinkAcademy.com